AF413148

ME AND THE MOTHER

ME AND THE MOTHER

LALITHA SAHASRANAMAM WITH CONTENT MEANING IN ENGLISH

Venkataraman Rajagopalan

Notion Press

Old No. 38, New No. 6
McNichols Road, Chetpet
Chennai - 600 031

First Published by Notion Press 2017
Copyright © Venkataraman Rajagopalan 2017
All Rights Reserved.

ISBN 978-1-946436-83-2
HC: 979-8-89475-508-3

Author Contact Details:
SPIRITUAL DIMENSIONS
126, Appar Swamy Koil St, Mylapore,
Chennai - 600004
Email: spiritualdimensions1942@gmail.com
Ph: 91-9840952777

About the Author......

Mr Venkataraman was born in Chennai in 1942, in a traditional bound family and is well versed in Sanskrit and other religious procedures. A post graduate in Instrument Technology from MIT, Chennai, he served in a British firm and in 1982, started his own instrument manufacture and system design. Blessed and initiated into Shreevidhya Upasana by great gurus at a young age, he also had the benefit of acquiring knowledge on such activities from his father, the renowned Sanskrit scholar Vazhuthur Rajagopala Sarma. He has been giving lectures on philosophy in an easily practiceable way in day to day life. He writes poems in Tamil, Sanskrit and articles in English. He was a visiting professor in MIT, Chennai.

Acknowledgements

I gratefully acknowledge the help from the following people in this endeavour (Vaak devathaa swaroopa iva)

- ❖ Baalaa Kaarunyaa Kumar for computer formatting and design.

- ❖ Smt. Krithika Radhakrishnan for giving the starting spark

- ❖ Smt Mala for helping in editing

- ❖ Smt. Gayathri Vijaykumar for script printing.

- ❖ Smt. Hema Venkataraman for suggestions on the grouping.

- ❖ Kumari Sarojini for computer typing.

- ❖ Sri SriHari for Sanskrit typing.

- ❖ Subhasri Vijayakumar

Preface

I got initiated into chanting of Lalitha Sahasranamam by my mother Srimati Balambal, Gayatri Mantra by my father Sri Vazhuthur Rajagopala Sarma, Veda patanam by Anna Sri N Subramania Iyer, and Sri Vidya mantropadesa by Srimathi Prabhavati Raje, a great devotee of Bhagawan Ramana Maharishi.

Maha Periyavaa gave Nayana Deeksha, Sadguru Gnanaananda gave Anna Deeksha and Seshadri Swamigal showed the great path. I am blessed to do saashtaanga namaskaram to all the Guru Mandala Devataaha. I feel their presence within me.

Recently, in Singapore, I participated in a group chanting of Lalitha Sahasranamam. **I explained the English meaning of a few slokas of the stotram which they could understand and appreciate well.** They were keen to get the entire meaning of Lalitha Sahasranamam in English. Hence they requested me to give the same in the form of a book which would be useful to them and for all those people who chant. I felt **this as a** stimulating spark coming from **the Divine Mother**. So I started writing the English meaning for every sloka giving the Tattvaartham (**content** / meaning) which **would inspire** the person who chants.Most of the translations available in the circulations are with word meaning or literal meaning which do not convey the inner experience of the sloka. Mother was putting all the words being penned down by me for the benefit of the chanting person.

There are only two sahasranamams commonly chanted everywhere namely that of Vishnu and Lalitha. Vishnu Sahasranamam **was** told by Bhishma to Pandavas whereas the Lalitha Sahasranamam **was** created by *Vak Devigal,* as ordained by Lalitha Parameshwari Herself and they formed the 1008 names of Lalitha.with each sloka interspersed with one letter of the fifteen letters Mantra (PANCHADASAAKSHARI). This unique feature gives the stotra **the** stature of **a** mantra.

Hence unlike Vishnu stotra, which can be chanted easily by anybody at anytime, Lalitha Sahasranamam, should be learnt from a Guru to learn with proper pronounciation. For this Sanskit knowledge is not essential. But we have to sit in a place and ignore all external diversions. **We have to put our effort to concentrate mentally on the** Mother whom we should start installing in our inner space deeper than our mind. This can be achieved by continuous effort.

Mind is capable of creating a simhasana/throne with **the** Mother seated on it. The Mother is fully ornamented with gold and precious stones. **She is dressed in red which matches the colour of her lips and wears garlands made of fragrant flowers.** All these can be construed in your mind with the worldly exposure you **already** have. **Your concentration will make it a virtual reality in your inner space.**

When you do a puja as guided by a shastrigal, a photo or idol of The Mother is placed in front of you. We should bring life into it for which PranaPratishta is performed. For this, we cleanse our soul inside us and **install** the same into the idol or photo in front of you.

This confirms that the Jeeva in you and the one installed in the idol are the same. Till the puja finishes, this single to dual concept should be **held. During** continuous practice you will realise that She is You and You are Her. **The Mother,** when seated in your Aatma Peeta, has Lakshmi on one side and Saraswati on the other side, which signifies SRI on one side and VIDYA on the other and **The Mother** is in the middle in the form of the Fifteen Letter Mantra. Thus Sri Vidya Upasana gets formed.

In my experience, I have seen several miraculous and unimaginable things happening to scores of people when they attend the puja. They come with their own problems and when they concentrate and pray, they find their problems identified and **getting solved, as The** Mother is present in live form during the Puja. This type of situation will happen regularly to you, if only you perform in the method mentioned as above in a natural fashion and procedure without worrying about the result. **The** Mother blesses people through your words and thought. This unique experience is available to all of you. With **The** Mother fully embedded **in** yourself, you will experience that you are becoming **a** different **person** - caring and **filled with compassion for others; having only** good words and thoughts for them.

While I did not write the meaning in any pre-planned manner, **I could feel Her Hand guiding me in forming the ideas and meaning which simply came out in a continuous flow.**

The sequence and content given in this book are as below:

1.   **Invoking** Her grace and blessings

2.   **Experiencing** Her grace visible through your actions and effects thereof.

3.   Your interactions with others

4.   You and others receive guidance and benefits

5.   She shows her **grace**

The meanings are easily applicable to all in their daily routines and also as guidance for **a satisfying** and successful future.

Through your **wholehearted practice**, people coming **in** contact with you will also smell and enjoy the fragrance ofand benefits.

Let us understand and realise that we are all one and the confirmation statement:

"I AM HER AND SHE IS ME"

श्री ललिता सहस्रनाम स्तोत्रम्॥

ध्यानम्

1. सिन्दूरारुणविग्रहां त्रिनयनां माणिक्यमौलिस्फुरत् I
   तारानायकशेखराम् स्मितमुखीमापीनवक्षोरुहाम् II

   Sindhooraaruna vigrahaam thri-nayanaam
   Maanikhya moulis**phurath**

   Thaaraanaayaka **sheka**raam **smitha**mukheem
   Aapeena-vakshoruhaam

2. पाणिभ्यामलिपूर्णरत्नचषकं रक्तोत्पलं बिभ्रतीं I
   सौम्याम् रथ्नघटस्थ रक्त चरणां ध्यायामि परां अम्बिकाम् II

   Paanibhyaam alipoorna ratnachashakam
   Raktothpalam bibhratheem

   Soumyaam rathnaghatastha raktha
   Charanaam dhyaayaami Paraam ambikaam

3. अरुणां करुणातरङ्गिताक्षीं धृत पाशाङ्कुश पुष्पबाणचापाम् I
अणिमादिभिः आवृतां मयूखैः अहमित्येव विभावये भवानीम्

Arunaam karunaa tharangithaaksheem
Dhrutha **paasha**ankusha pushpabaana
Chaapaam

Animaadhibi: **aav**ruthaam mayookai: aham
ithyeva vibhaavaye bhavaaneem

4. ध्यायामि पद्मासनस्थां विकसितवदनां पद्म पत्रायताक्षीं I
हेमाभां पीतवस्त्रां करकलितलसत् हेमपद्मां वराङ्गीम् II

Dhyaayaami padma aasanasthaam vikasitha
Vadhanaam padhma pathraayathaksheem

Hemaa**bhaam peetha**vasthraam
Karakalithalasath hemapadhmaam
Varaangeem

5.   सर्वालङ्कारयुक्तां सततमभयदां भक्तनम्रां भवानीं I
श्रीविद्यां शान्तमूर्ति सकलसुरनुतां सर्क्संपत् प्रदात्रीम् II

Sarvaalankaara yukthaam
Sathathamabhayadhaam Padhmanamraam
Bhavaaneem

Srividyhaam shanthamoorthim
Sakalasuranuthaam sarvasampath
Pradhaathreem

6.   सकुम्कुम विलेपनाम् अलिकचुम्बि कस्तूरिकां I
समन्द हसितेक्षणां सशरचाप पाशाङ्कुशाम् II

Sakumkuma vilepanaam alikachumbhi
Kasthoorikaam

Samantha hasithekshanaam sashara chaapa
Paashaankushaam

7. अशेष जनमोहिनीं अरुणमाल्यभूषाम्बरां ।
जपाकुसुमभासुरां जपविधौ स्मरामि अम्बिकाम् ॥

Asesha janamohineem arunamaalya
Bhooshaambaraam

Japaakusuma bhaasuraam japavidhou
Smaraami ambikaam

Dhyaana Sloka

When Dhyaana sloka is chanted, mindwise I must install The Mother on the Aatma Peetam, with description about **Her** bright **face,** adorned with all the ornaments studded with precious stones, **wearing kumkumam on the forehead and** flowers of high fragrance around her neck, clothes pure red **in** color matching her complexion, all these **are** brought to my mind based on my exposure to those various dress and ornament items in the outside world. I am now concentrating in my mind with The Mother **placed** in the seat of my soul.

Mother has pleasing and eye soothing brightness, eyes full of compassion and affection, holding in Her four hands *Bonding Rope, Bow and Arrow* made Sof sugar cane and flowers and **a controlling** metal tool *Ankusha* and *Abhaya Hastham.* She is surrounded by

Eight *Maha Siddhi devatas* who wield *chamarams*. I consider myself as HER since I am born to her. By Her side, I see Mahalakshmi seated on the lotus and holding **a lotus in each of her** hands with **an** assuring smile.

Now with Lakshmi on one side and Goddess Sarawathi on the other side, namely SRI on one side and VIDYA on the other side, making herself the *Mantra Swaroopini* in the middle by the *Panchadasi* Mantra, the whole concept of SRIVIDYA is enunciated. She makes the devotee fully rid of **fear and problems in life, shortage of wealth or lack** of affection. **She brings to her devotees love from all around and also makes them aspire for positive things and achieve them.**

I am fully convinced and **realise** that **YOU** are **Me** and **YOU** are blessing **Me** to show affection for all **and have granted me the power** of attracting all without any discrimination. This **knowledge engulfs** my mind.

(Please note that wherever in *Dhyana **Shloka**, Dhyaayeth* comes you must chant as *dhyaayaami* and *Smareth* as *smaraami*.)

The *Dhyaana **Shloka*** is not just for chanting. **A** sincerely involved prayer must accompany as follows:

"I installed **The** Mother in my *Aatma Peeta.* **The** Mother and Me are no longer two separate entities and hence whatever I work on, talk or think will be by Her through **me.**"

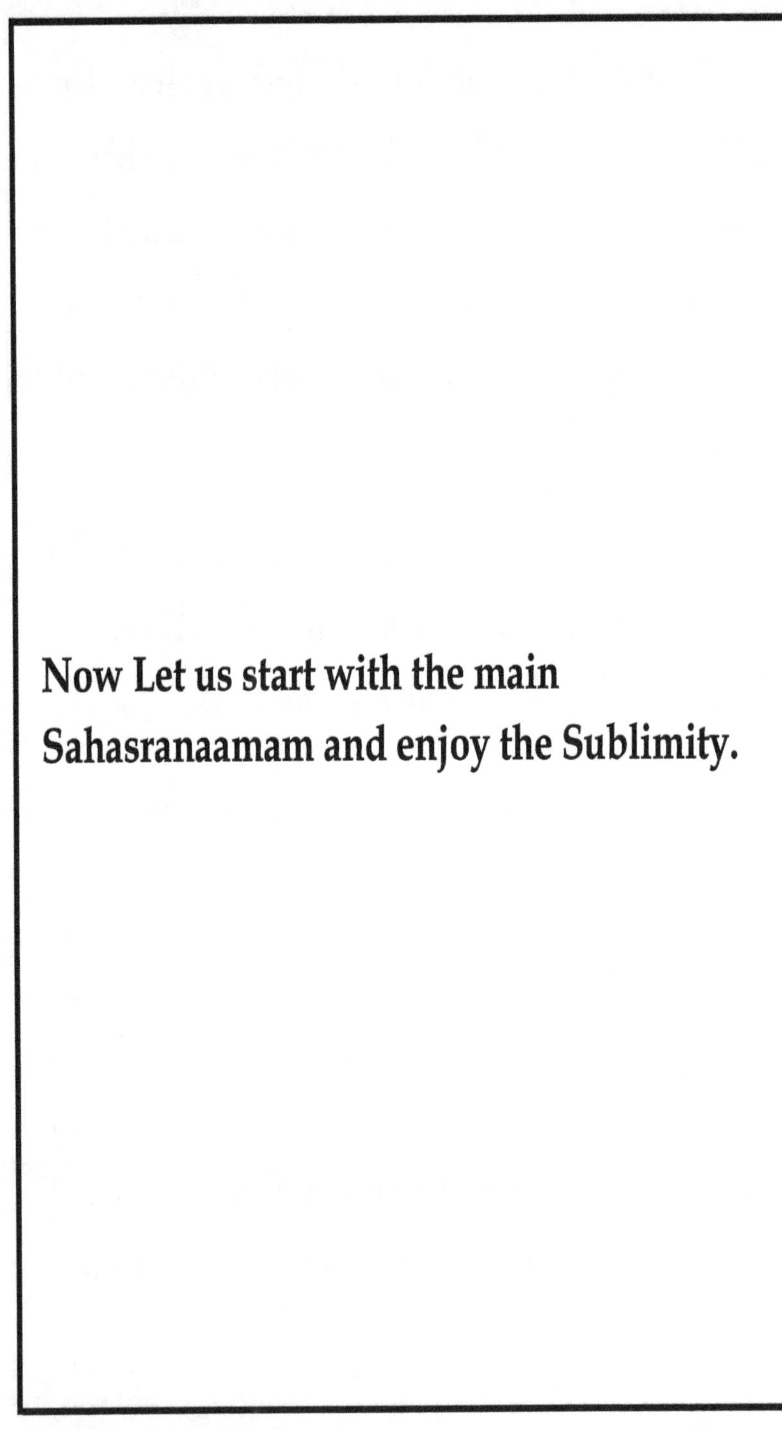

Now Let us start with the main Sahasranaamam and enjoy the Sublimity.

1

श्रीमाता श्रीमहाराज्ञी श्रीमत्सिंहासनेश्वरी ।
चिदग्नि-कुण्ड-सम्भूता देवकार्य-समुद्यता ॥ १ ॥

Shree Maatha shreemahaaraagyee
shreemath simhaasan**eshwaree**

Chithagni Kunda sambhootha
dhevakaarya samudhyathaa

Mother is embedded in my *Jiwa Peeta.* Her divine form has risen from my inner *Homa **Kunda*** to purify us from all our sins.

उद्यत्भानु -सहस्राभा चतुर्बाहु-समन्विता ।
रागस्वरूप पाशाढ्या क्रोधाकारा अन्कुशोज्ज्वला ॥२॥

Udyathbhaanu sahasraabhaa
chathurbaahu samanvithaa

Raagaswaroopa **paasha**adyaa
krodhaakaaraa ankushojwalaa

The Divine Mother blesses us with all her four hands and gives us brightness. Also she helps us overcome envy, anger, hunger and greed.

मनोरूपेक्षु-कोदण्डा पञ्चतन्मात्र-सायका ।

निजारुण-प्रभापूर- मज्जद्ब्रह्माण्ड -मण्डला ॥३॥

Manoroopekshu kodhandaa panchathan maathra saayakaa

Nijaaruna prabhaa poora majjadh brahmaanda mandalaa

The mind and the six *chakras* on the *kundalini* path are guided by Her and **the five *pranas* in the physical body are controlled by her.** Due to Her presence, we enjoy good health and vigour needed to be victorious in all our efforts.

चम्पकाशोक-पुन्नाग-सौगन्धिक-लसत्कचा ।
कुरुविन्दमणि-श्रेणी-कनत्कोटीर-मण्डिता ॥४

Champakaashoka punnaaga sougandhi
kalasath kachaa

Kuruvindha manishrenee kanathkoteera
mandithaa

The mother exudes floral fragrance and
eliminates the bad odour from inside us.
Dirt accumulated in our body through
our bad deeds and thoughts are washed
away. We transform into an ornament
studded with thousands of precious
stones.

अष्टमी चन्द्र- विभ्राज -दलिकस्थल-शोभिता ।
मुखचन्द्र -कलङ्काभ-मृगनाभि -विशेषका ॥५॥

Ashtamee chandhra vibhraaja
dhalikasthala shobitha

Mukhachandhra
kalangaabha mruganaabhi visheshakaa

The eighth moon imparts balanced light.
In a similar manner we will be able to
approach all our problems in a balanced
way with the blessings of the divine
form.

वदन्स्मर-माङ्गल्य-गृहतोरण- चिल्लिका ।
वक्त्रलक्ष्मी- परीवाह -चलन्मीनाभ-लोचना॥६॥

Vadhanasmara maangalya
gruhathoranachillikaa

Vakthralakshmee parivaaha chalan
meenaabha lochanaa

The Mother's face is beautiful and serene. In Her presence our home becomes auspicious, prosperous and festive. Mother blesses us with wealth and happiness.

नवचम्पक- पुष्पाभ- नासादण्ड-विराजिता ।

ताराकान्ति- तिरस्कारि नासाभरण- भासुरा ॥७॥

Navachampaka pushpaabha
naasaadhanda viraajithaa

Thaaraakaanthi thiraskaari
naasaabharana bhaasuraa

With deep inner devotion we can feel the freshness of the newly blossomed *Champaka* flower and the brightness of the light emanating from the ornament that adorns her nose.

(This reminds us of *Devi Kanyaakumari*)

कदम्बमञ्जरी-क्लृप्त-कर्णपूर-मनोहरा।
ताटङ्क-युगली-भूत-तपनोडुप-मण्डला॥८॥

Kadhamba manjaree kluptha karnapoora
manoharaa

Thaatanga yugaleebhootha thapanodupa
mandalaa

The Mother **wears** a garland of fragrant
flowers around her **neck**, ears sparkling
with the ornament *thaatangaa which*
imparts abundant energy to all parts of
our body (**reminds** us of *Akhilaandeswari
Amman* at *Tiruvaanaikoil*)

पद्मराग – शिलादर्श -परिभावि-कपोलभू:।

नवविद्रुम- बिम्बश्री -न्यक्कारि- रदनच्छदा॥९॥

Padhmaraaga **shila**adharsha paribhaavi kapolabhoo:

Navavidhruma bimbashree nyakkaaree ra**dhana**cchhadhaa

The two sides of her face act like reflective mirrors for us to **see**, evaluate and modify our actions and improve ourselves. The two lips which look like beautiful coral shells remind us to **refrain** from speaking harsh words to others.

शुद्धविद्यांकुराकार-द्विजपंक्ति-द्वयोज्ज्वला।
कर्पूरवीटिकामोद-समाकर्षि-दिगन्तरा ॥१०॥

Shuddhavidhyaankuraakaara
dhwijapankthi **dvayoj**walaa

Karpooraveetikaamodha samaakarshi
dhigantharaa

The Mother's teeth **are glaring** in whiteness, 16 in each **at** the top and the bottom with jaws at the end joining them. It represents the 16 *bheejaksharams* coming in the *Shodasi*. Her blessings attract learned and ignorant people towards Her **as they focus their concentration** on Her.

निज-सल्लाप-माधुर्य- विनिर्भर्त्सित -कच्छपी ।
मन्दस्मित -प्रभापूर-मज्जत्कामेश-मानसा॥११॥

Nijasallaapa maadhurya vinirbhartsitha **Kachcha**pee

Mandhasmitha prabhapoora majjadhkaamesha maanasaa

She blesses you with an attractive voice making everybody to get interested in listening to your voice and its content. Your smile drives away all their problems **and makes** them happy.

अनाकलित -सादृश्य- चिबुकश्री-विराजिता।

कामेश-बद्ध-माङ्गल्य-सूत्र-शोभित-कन्धरा ॥१२॥

Anaakalitha saadhrusya chibhukashree viraajithaa

Kaamesha baddha maangalya soothra shobhitha kandharaa

Her precise and beautiful chin ensures that **your work would be exact and perfect for your needs with effective outcomes**. Your married life will be satisfying and happy to all concerned.

कनकाङ्गद- केयूर- कमनीय- भुजान्विता।
रत्नग्रैवेय-चिन्ताक-लोल-मुक्ता- फलान्विता ॥१३॥

Kanakaangadha keyoora kamaneeya bhujaanvithaa

Rathnagraiveya chinthaaka lolamukthaa phalaanvithaa

She wears bangles and special ornaments **in Her** fore arms. They consist of various precious stones and metals just to show that all varieties of people are guided by Her which they will realise if they see Her within themselves.

कामेश्वर-प्रेमरत्न-मणि-प्रतिपण-स्तनी ।

नाभ्यालवाल – रोमालि -लता-फलकुचद्वयी ॥१४॥

Kaameshwara premarathna mani
prathipana sthanee

Naabhyaala vaalaromaali lathaaphala
kuchadhwayee

Just like Breastmilk is good for child for
good growth, knowledge and health, **She**
blesses you with Her breastfeeding
which gives you energy and activates the
areas like stomach, heart and chest into
proper functioning. (**This** reminds us of
Saint Tirugyaanasambandhar).

लक्ष्यरोम-लताधारता-समुन्नेय-मध्यमा ।
स्तनभार-दलन्मध्य- पट्टबन्ध-वलित्रया ॥१५॥

Lakshyaroma lathaa dhaarathaa
samunneya madhyamaa

Sthana bhaara dalanmadhya
pattabandha valithrayaa

By concentrating on **the** different parts of
her body, as conceived in your mind, you
will find all your most difficult objectives
fulfilled. Her motherly affection has no
boundary in providing prosperity to you.

अरुणारुणकौसुम्भ-वस्त्र-भास्वत्-कटीतटी ।
रत्न- किङ्किणिका-रम्य-रशना-दाम-भूषिता ॥१६॥

Arunaaruna kousumbha
vastrabhaaswath kateethatee

Ratnakinkinikaa ramya rashanaa
dhaamabhooshitaa

Her presence inside you helps you to
dress appropriately and she ensures that
you utter meaningful words which
sound as soothing as one coming from
chiming **bells.**

कामेश-ज्ञात-सौभाग्य-मार्दवोरु-द्वयान्विता ।
माणिक्य- मुकुटाकार -जानुद्वय-विराजिता ॥१७॥

Kaamesha gnyaatha sowbhaagya
maardhavoru dhwayaanvithaa

Maanikya mukutaakaara jaanudhwaya
viraajithaa

The Mother fulfills all your desires and
blesses you with eternal prosperity. She
blesses you with ornaments and gold
studded with valuable diamonds and
stones.

इन्द्रगोप-परिक्षिप्त- स्मरतूणाभ - जंघिका ।
गूढगुल्फा कूर्मपृष्ठ-जयिष्णु- प्रपदान्विता ॥१८॥

Indhragopa parikshiptha
smarathoonaabha jhangikaa

Gooda**gulphaa** koormaprushtaa jayishnu
prapadhaanvithaa

She enables you to overcome any hardships and protects you against mental or physical affliction.

नख-दीधिति-संछन्न-नमज्जन-तमोगुणा ।
पदद्वय-प्रभाजाल-पराकृत-सरोरुहा ॥१९॥

Nakha dee**dhithi sam**channa namajjana thamo gunaa

Padhadhwaya prabhaa jaala **paraa**krutha saroruhaa

You will receive strength to overcome laziness and be joyfully active. You will keep the place pure and fragrant.

सिञ्जान-मणिमञ्जीर-मण्डित-श्री- पदाम्बुजा

मराली-मन्दगमना-महालावण्य-शेवधिः ॥२०॥

Sinjaana manimanjeera **mandi**thashree
padhaambhujaa

Maraalee mandhagamanaa
Mahaalaavanya sevadhi:

Your place will be filled with divine
fragrance, prosperity and wealth.

सर्वारुणाऽनवद्याङ्गी-सर्वाभरण-भूषिता ।
शिव-कामेश्वराङ्कस्था- शिवा- स्वाधीन-वल्लभा ॥२१॥

Sarvaarunaa – anavadhyaangee-
sarvaabharana bhooshithaa

Shiva kaameswaraankasthaa **shivaa**
swaadheena vallabhaa

All parts of your body will function
efficiently and you will enjoy good health
and a peaceful and harmonious family
life.

सुमेरु-मध्य-शृङ्गस्था श्रीमन्नगर-नायिका ।
चिन्तामणि गृहान्तस्था पञ्च-ब्रह्मासन-स्थिता ॥२२॥

Sumeru madhya srungasthaa shreeman nagara naayikaa

Chinthaamani gruhaantasthaa pancha brahmaasana sthithaa

You will be deemed as the leader amongst groups and will gradually attain **an** invincible position in your field of work. You will reside in a place which has fresh air, clean water, bright sunshine and fertile land which brings you peace.

महापद्माटवी-संस्था कदम्बवन-वासिनी ।
सुधासागर-मध्यस्था कामाक्षी कामदायिनी ॥२३॥

Mahaapadhmaatavee samsthaa
kadhambha vana vaasinee

Sudhasaagara madhyasthaa
kaamaakshee kamadhaayinee

You will gain recognition worldwide in
the chosen field of work. People will seek
your advice after seeing your progress.

देवर्षि- गण -संघात- स्तूयमानात्म-वैभवा ।
भण्डासुर-वधोद्युक्त-शक्तिसेना-समन्विता ॥२४॥

Devarshi gana sanghaatha
sthooyamaanaathma vaibhavaa

Bhandaasura vadhothyuktha
shakthisenaa samanvithaa

You will get to see the Mother and feel Her presence. You will have the blessings of Saints to overcome hurdles and still have abundant energy.

सम्पत्करी-समारूढ- सिंधुर -व्रज-सेविता ।
अश्वारूढाधिष्टिताश्व -कोटि-कोटिभि-रावृता॥ २५॥

Sampathkaree samaarooda sindhoora vrajasevithaa

Ashwaaroodaadhishtidhaaswa koti kotibhiraavruthaa

You will have company of good peers who will contribute positively towards your growth and prosperity.

चक्रराज-रथारूढ-सर्वायुध-परिष्कृता ।
गेयचक्र-रथारूढ मन्त्रिणी -परिसेविता ॥२६॥

Chakraraaja rathaarooda sarvaayudha parishkruthaa

Geyachakra rathaarooda mantrinee parisevithaa

In your presence humans will stop violence, shun negative **behavior,** realise peace and also change their path to righteousness.

किरिचक्ररथारूढ-दण्डनाथा-पुरस्कृता ।
ज्वालामालिनिकाक्षिप्त-वह्निप्राकार-मध्यगा ॥२७॥

Kirichakra rathaarooda dhandanaathaa
puras**kruthaa**

Jwalaamalinikaa kshiptha
vahnipraakaara madhyagaa

Just as things put in the fire vanish, all aberrations and errors get consumed in the fire inside **you,** thanks to Her blessings.

भण्डसैन्य-वधोद्युक्त-शक्ति-विक्रम-हर्षिता ।
नित्या- पराक्रमाटोप-निरीक्षण-समुत्सुका ॥२८॥

Bhandasainya vadhothyuktha **shakthi**
vikrama harshithaa

Nithyaa paraakramaatopa nireekshana
samuthsukaa

After you overcome your negativity you
will have the confidence to perform your
activity with full vigour and enthusiasm.

भण्डपुत्र -वधोद्युक्त –बाला-विक्रम-नन्दिता ।
मन्त्रिण्यम्बा- विरचित -विषङ्ग-वध-तोषिता॥२९॥

Bhandhaputhra vadhothyuktha baalaa vikrama nandithaa

Manthrinyambaa virachitha vishanga vadhathoshithaa

You will destroy all invisible demons in your mind and also remove dangerous conditions from any part of your body thanks to Her blessings.

विशुक्र-प्राणहरण-वाराही-वीर्य-नन्दिता ।
कामेश्वर-मुखालोक-कल्पित-श्रीगणेश्वरा ॥३०॥

Visukra praana harana vaaraahee veerya nandhithaa

Kaameswara mukhaaloka kalpitha shreeganeshwaraa

You will bring out the most satisfying and innovative products by combined power of your mind and knowledge. This will put an end to old practices for similar utility. This particularly applies to your puja methods.

महागणेश-निर्भिन्न-विघ्नयन्त्र-प्रहर्षिता
भण्डासुरेन्द्र-निर्मुक्त-शस्त्रप्रत्यस्त्र-वर्षिणी ॥३१॥

Mahaaganesha nirbhinna vignayanthra praharshithaa

Bhandhaasurendra nirmuktha **shasthra** prathyastra varshinee

You will crush all obstacles and impediments and march forward with confidence since She has blessed you to **successfully overcome** your mental and physical diffidence.

कराङ्गुलि-नखोत्पन्न- नारायण दशाकृतिः।
महा- पाशुपतास्त्राग्नि-निर्दग्धासुर-सैनिका ॥३२॥

Karaanguli nakhothpanna naraayana
dhashaakrithihi:

Mahaa paashupathaasthraagni
nirdhagdhaasura sainikaa

Mother holds your hand for taking on
any activity with practical and serene
approach bringing success after burning
off ignorance by **the** fire of your
knowledge.

कामेश्वरास्त्र-निर्दग्ध- सभण्डासुर -शून्यका ।
ब्रह्मोपेन्द्र -महेन्द्रादि-देव-संस्तुत-वैभवा॥३३॥

Kaameshwaraasthra nirdhagdha
sabhandaasura shoonyakaa

Brahmopendhra mahendhraadhi dheva
samsthutha vaibhavaa

You will receive praise from one and all
for your approach and effort to eliminate
problems and thereby provide solutions
for mental and physical blocks.

हर-नेत्राग्नि-संदग्ध-काम-सञ्जीवनौषधिः ।
श्रीमद्वाग्भव-कूटैक-स्वरूप-मुख-पङ्कजा॥३४॥

Hara nethraagni samdhagdha kaama
sanjeevanoushadhi:

Shreemadhvaakbhava kootaika
swaroopa mukha pankajaa

By Her grace, bad effects due to others'
jealousy over your achievements in your
chosen field will not affect you. Also you
will have better clarity and brightness.

कण्ठाधः कटि-पर्यन्त-मध्यकूट-स्वरूपिणी ।
शक्तिकूटैकतापन्न-कट्यधोभाग-धारिणी ॥३५॥

Kanthaadhah katiparyantha madhyakoota swaroopinee

Shakthikootai kathaapanna katyadhobhaaga dhaarinee

When you recognise Her to be in you She blesses you through benevolent words emanating from Her *naabhi,* then through the chest and heart portion and then through the throat and Her mouth. That is the result of Kundalini energy passing through the relevant chakras giving corresponding energy effects.

मूलमन्त्रात्मिका मूलकूटत्रय- कलेबरा ।
कुलामृतैक-रसिका-कुलसंकेत-पालिनी ॥३६॥

Moolamanthraathmikaa
moolakootathraya kalebharaa

Kulaamruthaika rasikaa kulasanketha
paalinee

All activities will fail when conducted in an agitated mind. She protects you through your parents and forefathers to bless you to get into **a state of** calmness.

कुलाङ्गना कुलान्तस्था कौलिनी कुलयोगिनी ।
अकुला समयान्तस्था समयाचार-तत्परा ॥३७॥

Kulaanganaakulaanthasthaa kaulinee kulayoginee

Akulaa samayaanthasthaa samayaachaara thathparaa

When the blessings of your parents and forefathers are coupled with Her grace, it will keep you in the right path always.

मूलाधारैक-निलया-ब्रह्मग्रन्थि-विभेदिनी ।
मणिपूरान्तरुदिता विष्णुग्रन्थि-विभेदिनी ॥३८॥

Moolaadharaika nilayaa brahmagranthi
vibhedhinee

Manipooraantha rudhithaa
vishnugranthi vibhedhinee

She is the single source who can remove
all your knotty problems from birth to
present **time** - in every activity and
livelihood of yours.

आज्ञाचक्रान्तरालस्था रुद्रग्रन्थि-विभेदिनी।
सहस्राराम्बुजारूढा सुधासाराभिवर्षिणी ॥३९॥

Aagyachakraantaraalasthaa rudhra
granthi vibhedhinee

Sahasraara ambhujaaroodaa
sudhaasaaraabhi varshinee

She unties the knot of fear of accidents
and mishaps or death of your near and
dear. By Her grace all your actions will
command respect since you imbibe good
habits, culture and knowledge. That
effect results in continuous flow of
immense happiness.

तडिल्लता समरुचिः षट्चक्रोपरि -संस्थिता।
महाशक्तिः कुण्डलिनी बिसतन्तु -तनीयसी ॥४०॥

Thadillathaa samaruchihee
shatchakropari samsthithaa

Mahaashakthihee kundalinee
bhisathanthu thaneeyasee

You will perform your work with full involvement because of your mental control of all the six *gunaas*.

भवानी भावनागम्या भवारण्य-कुठारिका ।
भद्रप्रिया भद्रमूर्ति-भक्त-सौभाग्यदायिनी ॥४१॥

Bhavaanee **bhaava**naa gamyaa
bhavaaranya kutaarikaa

Bhadhrapriyaa bhadhra moorthi:
bhaktha sowbhaagya dhaayinee

She blesses you a future full of good and enjoyable surroundings along with prosperity and good health. You will have humility and share your prosperity with those in need.

भक्तिप्रिया भक्तिगम्या भक्तिवश्या भयापहा ।
शाम्भवी शारदाराध्या शर्वाणी शर्मदायिनी॥४२॥

Bhakthipriyaa bhakthigamyaa
bhathi**vashyaa** bhayaapahaa

Shaambhavee shaaradhaaraadhyaa
sharvaanee sharmadhaayinee

She is pleased with your realisation of identity with Her. Your future is bright and you will be held in high esteem with due respect and affection.

43

शाङ्करी श्रीकरी साध्वी शरत्चंद्र – निभानना ।

शातोदरी शान्तिमती निराधारा निरञ्जना ॥४३॥

Shaankaree shreekaree saadhwee sharadhchandra nibhaananaa

Shaathodharee shaanthimathee niraadhaaraa niranjanaa

You will be blessed to have crystal clear mind like the moon in the winter, peace and wealth accrued by your hard work and you will lend support to others. You will enjoy a relaxed and peaceful mind.

निर्लेपा निर्मला नित्या निराकारा निराकुला ।
निर्गुणा निष्कला शान्ता निष्कामा निरुपप्लवा ॥४४॥

Nirlepaa nirmalaa nithyaa niraakaaraa niraakulaa

Nirgunaa nishkalaa shaanthaa nishkaamaa nirupaplavaa

You will view everything in a larger perspective and avoid the narrow vision of 'me and mine'.

नित्यमुक्ता निर्विकारा निष्प्रपञ्चा निराश्रया ।
नित्यशुद्धा नित्यबुद्धा निरवद्या निरन्तरा ॥४५॥

Nithyamukthaa nirvikaaraa
nish**prapanchaa** niraashrayaa

Nithyashuddhaa nityabhuddhaa
niravadhyaa nirantharaa

The Mother makes you totally free of all bad thoughts in your life which is possible by Her alone since she is goodness and purity personified.

निष्कारणा निष्कलङ्का निरुपाधि-निरीश्वरा ।
नीरागा रागमथनी निर्मदा मदनाशिनी ॥४६॥

Nishkaaranaa nishkalankaa
niruphaadhir nireeshwara

Neeraagaa raagamathanee nirmadhaa
madha**naashinee**

निश्चिन्ता निरहङ्कारा निर्मोहा मोहनाशिनी ।
निर्ममा ममताहन्त्री निष्पापा पापनाशिनी ॥४७॥

Nischinthaa nirahankaaraa nirmohaa
mohanaashinee

Nirmamaa mamathaahanthree
nishpaapaa paapanaashinee

निष्क्रोधा क्रोधशमनी निर्लोभा लोभनाशिनी ।
निःसंशया संशयघ्नी निर्भवा भवनाशिनी ॥४८॥

Nishkrodhaa krodhashamanee nirlobhaa lobhanaashinee

Nissamshayaa samshayagnee nirbhavaa bhava naashinee

निर्विकल्पा निराबाधा निर्भेदा भेदनाशिनी ।
निर्नाशा मृत्युमथनी निष्क्रिया निष्परिग्रहा ॥४९॥

Nirvikalpaa niraabhaadhaa nirbhedhaa bhedha naashinee

Nirnaashaa mruthyu mathanee nishkriyaa nishparigrahaa

निस्तुला नीलचिकुरा निरपाया निरत्यया ।
दुर्लभा दुर्गमा दुर्गा दुःखहन्त्री सुखप्रदा ॥५०॥

Nisthulaa neela chikuraa nirapaayaa nirathyayaa

Dhurlabhaa dhurgamaa dhurgaa dhukha hanthree sukhapradhaa

Only learned people can remove our ignorance. The Mother's various qualities in complete fullness remove our deficiency in any quality since you have recognised that you have Her genes.

दुष्टदूरा दुराचारशमनी दोष-वर्जिता ।
सर्वज्ञा सान्द्र करुणा समानाधिक-वर्जिता ॥५१॥

Dhushtadhooraa dhuraachaara
shamanee dhoshavarjithaa

Sarvagyaa saandhrakarunaa
samaanaadhika varjithaa

All miseries and sorrow will be away
from you by Her grace. You will live
without any blemish. You will be
compassionate and sympathetic to all.

सर्वशक्तिमयी सर्वमङ्गला सद्गति-प्रदा ।
सर्वेश्वरी सर्वमयी सर्वमन्त्रस्वरूपिणी ॥५२॥

Sarvashakthimayee sarvamangalaa
sathgathipradhaa

Sarveshwaree sarvamayee sarvamanthra
swaroopinee

You will be full of energy and you will
have an affectionate approach towards
all beings and you **will** guide them
towards the right path. With a well
balanced mind you will make **yourself**
easily accessible.

सर्वयन्त्रात्मिका सर्व-तन्त्ररूपा-मनोन्मनी ।
माहेश्वरी महादेवी महालक्ष्मी .-मृडप्रिया ॥५३॥

Sarvayanthraathmikaa sarva
thanthraroopaa manonmanee

Maaheshwaree mahaadevee
mahaalakshmee: mrudapriyaa

You become aware of the external and
internal movements of the body and the
mind when you chant towards Her with
mental concentration. Your poise and
balance provide happiness and wealth to
all.

महारूपा महापूज्या महा-पातक-नाशिनी ।
महामाया महासत्त्वा महाशक्ति-महारतिः ॥५४॥

Mahaaroopaa mahaapujyaa mahaa **paathaka**naashinee

Mahaamaayaa mahaasathwaa mahaashakthi: mahaarathi:

People respect you **in society** for your immense and effective energy and calmness. Hence people around you shun violence and stick to your path of calmness and balance.

महाभोगा महैश्वर्या महावीर्या महाबला ।
महाबुद्धि-महासिद्धि-महायोगेश्वरेश्वरी ॥५५॥

Mahaabhogaa mahaishwaryaa mahaaveeryaa mahaabhalaa

Mahaabhuddhir Mahaasiddhir mahaayogeshwareshwaree

Mother blesses you with good health and wealth. She blesses you to achieve your goals through your extraordinary knowledge and unification of all your capabilities.

महातन्त्रा महामन्त्रा महायन्त्रा महासना ।
महायाग-क्रमाराध्या महाभैरव-पूजिता ॥५६॥

Mahaa thanthraa mahaa manthraa
mahaa yanthraa mahaasanaa

Mahaa yaaga kramaaraadhyaa
mahaabhairava pujithaa

Your mental planning and meticulous executions take you to high levels. Your creative thinking, attractive oratorical capabilities and systematic working make people look at you with admiration.

महेश्वर-महाकल्प-महाताण्डव -साक्षिणी ।
महाकामेश-महिषी महात्रिपुरसुन्दरी ॥५७॥

Maheshwara mahaakalpa
mahaathaandava saakshinee

Mahaakaamesha mahishee mahaa
thripurasundharee

You will adapt to different situations to achieve your goals without sacrificing the values you cherish and by conforming to your principles.

चतुष्षष्ट्युपचाराढ्या चतुष्षष्टिकलामयी ।
महाचतुः -षष्टिकोटि-योगिनी-गणसेविता ॥५८॥

Chathushashti upacha**araadyaa**
chathushshasti kalaamayee

Mahaachathu: shashtikotee yoginee
ganasevithaa

While there are multiple ways of devotion and prayers and mental concentration, you will adopt the simple way of identifying yourself with Her, whom you have installed in your *Athma Peetam.*

मनुविद्या चन्द्रविद्या चन्द्रमण्डल-मध्यगा ।
चारुरूपा चारुहासा चारुचन्द्र-कलाधरा ॥५९॥

Manu vidhyaa Chandhra vidhyaa
Chandhra mandala madhyagaa

Chaaruroopaa chaaruhaasaa
chaaruchandra kalaadharaa

This type of puja is brought in practice by great saints and sages. Hence this is the proper way of performing the Puja.

चराचर-जगन्नाथा चक्रराज-निकेतना ।
पार्वती पद्मनयना पद्म राग समप्रभा ॥६०॥

Charaachara jagannaathaa chakraraaja nikethanaa

Paarvathee padhmanayanaa padhmaraaga samaprabhaa

Your mind will first analyse the effectiveness of association or dissociation of activities without extraneous control but in a natural way which is the main reason for great achievements.

पञ्चप्रेतासनासीना पञ्चब्रह्मस्वरूपिणी ।
चिन्मयी परमानन्दा विज्ञानघनरूपिणी ॥६१॥

Panchapretha aasanaaseenaa pancha
brahma swaroopinee

Chinmayee paramaanandhaa vigyaana
Ghana roopinee

You will be one with nature and also control the five functional parts of the body which are essential for external connections and communications. Because of your analytical mind, you will experience eternal bliss forever.

ध्यान-ध्यातृ-ध्येयरूपा धर्माधर्म-विवर्जिता ।
विश्वरूपा जागरिणी स्वपन्ती तैजसात्मिका ॥६२॥

Dhyaana dhyaathru dhyeyaroopaa
dharmaadharma vivarjitha

Viswaroopa jaagarinee swapanthee
thaijasaathmikaa

You perform all the activities as ordained
by Her and hence the result will be
excellent. You **will benefit** and shine.

सुप्ता प्राज्ञात्मिका तुर्या सर्वावस्था-विवर्जिता ।
सृष्टिकर्त्री ब्रह्मरूपा गोप्त्री गोविन्दरूपिणी ॥६३॥

Supthaa praagyathmikaa thuryaa
sarvaavasthaa vivarjithaa

Srushtikarthree brahmaroopa gopthree
govindharoopinee

You are blessed to awake from slumber, sleep, deep sleep and other latent States and make you active and creative. You will advise people from children onwards the importance of realising the outwardly invisible presence of Her.

संहारिणी रुद्ररूपा तिरोधानकरीश्वरी ।
सदाशिवाऽनुग्रहदा पञ्चकृत्यपरायणा ॥६४॥

Samhaarinee rudhraroopaa thirodhaana
kareeswaree

Sadhaashiva anugrahadha
panchakruthya paraayanaa

You will overcome all evil energies and
those obstructing the path of perfection.
You will be above all attachments and do
justice to the relationships.

भानुमण्डल-मध्यस्था भैरवी भगमालिनी ।
पद्मासना भगवती पद्मनाभ-सहोदरी ॥६५॥

Bhaanumandala madhyasthaa bhairavee bhagamaalinee

Padhmaasanaa bhagavathee padhmanaabha sahodharee

She removes the excess heat in you, caused by emotions, anger, and physical heat and keeps you calm and cool to concentrate deeply on your activity. You will guide people to gain wealth in a proper and rightful manner.

उन्मेष-निमिषोत्पन्न-विपन्न-भुवनावली ।
सहस्रशीर्षवदना सहस्राक्षी सहस्रपात् ॥६६॥

Unmesha nimishothpanna vipanna
bhuvanaavalee

Sahasraseershavadhanaa sahasraakshee
sahasrapaath

You are blessed to attend to the
individual requirements of people and
you provide permanent solutions. People
strive for temporary solutions which are
never long lasting.

आब्रह्म-कीट-जननी वर्णाश्रम-विधायिनी ।
निजाज्ञारूप-निगमा पुण्यापुण्य-फलप्रदा ॥६७॥

Aabrahma keetajananee varnaashrama vidhaayinee

Nijaagyaa roopnigamaa punyaapunya phalapradhaa

With millions of people having the same Jeeva but in different and varied structures, each has a specific role to play and you are in a position to see the do's and dont's of every single activity.

श्रुति-सीमन्त-सिन्दूरी-कृत-पादाब्ज़धूलिका ।
सकलागम-सन्दोह-शुक्ति-सम्पुट-मौक्तिका ॥६८॥

Shruthi seemantha sindhooree krutha
paadhabhja dhoolikaa

Sakalaagama sandhoha shukthi samputa
moukthikaa

You understand and share with others
the righteous way to function, the right
time to function with respect to the
present time.

पुरुषार्थ-प्रदा पूर्णा भोगिनी भुवनेश्वरी ।
अम्बिकाऽनादि-निधना हरिब्रह्मेन्द्र-सेविता॥६९॥

Purushaarthapradhaa poornaa bhoginee
bhuvaneshwaree

Ambikaa anaadhi nidhanaa hari
brammendhra sevithaa

Though you are blessed with vast wealth
and happiness due to Her Grace, you will
help others who are drawn to you
because of your positive approach.

नारायणी नादरूपा नामरूप विवर्जिता ।
ह्रींकारी ह्रीमती हृद्या हेयोपादेय-वर्जिता ॥७०॥

Naaraayanee Naadharoopaa
Naamaroopa vivarjithaa

Hreemkaaree hreemathee hrudhyaa
heyopaadheya varjithaa

You will be surrounded by people doing
bhajans and you will experience Oneness
with Her and show them the reality and
the permanent truth.

राजराजार्चिता राज्ञी रम्या राजीव-लोचना ।
रञ्जनी रमणी रस्या रणत्किङ्किणि-मेखला ॥७१॥

Rajaraajaarchithaa raagyee ramyaa
rajeeva lochanaa

Ranjanee ramanee rasyaa ranath kinkini
mekhalaa

Leaders will seek your guidance or assistance. They experience joy and happiness when you are nearby. They see your total commitment and involvement in your assignments.

रमा राकेन्दु-वदना रतिरूपा रतिप्रिया ।
रक्षाकरी राक्षसघ्नी रामा रमणलम्पटा ॥७२॥

Ramaa rakendhu vadhanaa rathiroopaa rathipriyaa

Rakshaakaree raakshasagnee raamaa ramanalampataa

You will by Her grace, advise on how to obtain wealth and happiness in the proper manner. You will teach people how to retain wealth and use their wealth in a beneficial way.

काम्या कामकलारूपा कदम्ब -कुसुम-प्रिया ।
कल्याणी जगती-कन्दा करुणा-रस-सागरा ॥७३॥

Kaamyaa kaamakalaa roopaa
kadhambha kusumapriyaa

Kalyaanee jagathee kandhaa karunaa
rasa saagaraa

You will guide people to have happy and
harmonious married life which will give
them peace and sanctity in their home.

कलावती कलालापा कान्ता कादम्बरी प्रिया ।
वरदा वामनयना वारुणी मदविह्वला ॥७४॥

Kalaavathee kalaalaapaa kaanthaa
kaadhambaree priyaa

Varadhaa vaamanayanaa vaarunee
madhavihwalaa

You find joy in using your knowledge to benefit others. You communicate effectively on any subject, share information and provide guidance so that people too can achieve perfection in their life.

विश्वाधिका वेदवेद्या विन्द्याचल-निवासिनी ।
विधात्री वेदजननी विष्णुमाया विलासिनी॥७५॥

Vishwaadhikaa vedhavedhyaa
vindhyaachala nivaasinee

Vidhaathree vedhajananee
vishnumaayaa vilaasinee

Through your acquaintance people overcome ignorance and acquire pure knowledge on worldly matters and aim for that ultimate truth.

क्षेत्रस्वरूपा क्षेत्रेशी क्षेत्र-क्षेत्रज्ञ-पालिनी ।
क्षय वृद्धि -विनिर्मुक्ता क्षेत्रपाल-समर्चिता ॥७६॥

Kshethraswaroopaa kshethreshee
kshethra kshethragya paalinee

Kshayavruddhi vinirmukthaa
kshethrapaala samarchithaa

You will maintain your body and mind
in a good and healthy way and by proper
monitoring and control you will
eliminate unwanted, negative growth or
decay.

विजया विमला वन्द्या वन्दारु-जनवत्सला ।
वाग्वादिनी वामकेशी वह्निमण्डल-वासिनी ॥७७॥

Vijayaa vimalaa vandhyaa vandhaaru janavathsalaa

Vaakvaadhinee vaamakeshee vahnimandala vaasinee

You will receive appreciative recognition from all quarters and your way of explaining to people will be liked by them to pursue further.

भक्तिमत् कल्पलतिका पशुपाश-विमोचिनी ।
संहृताशेष - पाषण्डा सदाचार – प्रवर्तिका ॥७८॥

Bhakthimath kalpalathikaa pashupaasha
vimochinee

Samhruthaasesha paashandhaa
sadhaachaara pravarthikaa

You rejoice when people also strive to
obtain true realisation after destroying
old concept of prayers. Now they firmly
believe in good and strong procedures.

तापत्रयाग्नि- सन्तप्त-समाह्लादन-चन्द्रिका ।
तरूणी तापसाराध्या तनुमध्या तमोपहा ॥७९॥

Thaapathrayaagni santhaptha
samaahlaadhana chandhrikaa

Tharunee thaapasaaraadhyaa
thanumadhyaa thamopahaa

People get relief from misery and learn to
lead the middle path without getting
affected by gaiety or anxiety because of
the blessings of Mother.

चिति-स्तत्पद-लक्ष्यार्था चिदेकरस-रूपिणी ।

स्वात्मानन्द -लवीभूत-ब्रह्मााद्यानन्द-सन्ततिः ॥८०॥

Chithispadha lakshyaarthaa
chidhekarasa roopinee

Swathmaanandha laveebhootha
brahmaadhyaanandha santhathi:

All this is possible by you because of the mental concentration on Her, who is seated in you. You will derive unparalleled satisfaction for yourself and to all others.

परा प्रत्यक्-चितीरूपा पश्यन्ती परदेवता ।
मध्यमा वैखरी-रूपा-भक्त-मानस-हंसिका ॥८१॥

Paraa prathyak chitheeroopaa
pashyanthee paradhevathaa

Madhyamaa vaikhareeroopaa bhaktha
maanasa hamsikaa

You will be mentally formulating any
product, executing it aesthetically and
you spread the knowledge to various
levels of learned to ignorant people and
delight them with the invention.

कामेश्वर-प्राणनाडी कृतज्ञा कामपूजिता ।
शृङ्गार-रस-संपूर्णा जया जालन्धर-स्थिता ॥८२॥

Kaameshwara praananaadee
kruthagnyaa kaamapoojithaa

Shrungaara rasa sampoornaa jayaa
jaalandharasthithaa

With Her blessings you will master any
subject and make a product which will be
excellent, attractive and bring you glory
and victory.

ओड्याण-पीठ-निलया बिन्दु-मण्डलवासिनी ।
रहोयाग-क्रमाराध्या-रहस्तर्पण-तर्पिता ॥८३॥

Odyaana peeta nilayaa bindhumandala
vaasinee

Rahoyaaga kramaaraadhyaa
rahastharpana tharpithaa

You will not get pulled into vicious
circles but will reach the depths of
research and development without
publicity. The final product will
command high utility and admiration.

सद्यःप्रसादिनी विश्व साक्षिणी साक्षि वर्जिता ।
षडङ्गदेवता-युक्ता षाड्गुण्य -परिपूरिता ॥८४॥

Sadhya: prasaadhinee viswa saakshinee saakshi varjithaa

Shadanga devathaayukthaa shaadgunya paripoorithaa

You will achieve ultimate success noticed by the world with all your senses acting in harmony by Her grace.

नित्य- क्लिन्ना निरुपमा निर्वाण-सुख-दायिनी ।
नित्याषोडशिका-रूपा श्रीकण्ठार्ध-शरीरिणी॥८५॥

Nithyaklinnaa mirupamaa nirvaana
sukha dhaayinee

Nityaa shodashikaaroopaa
shrikantaardha sareerinee

She makes you humble and full of
compassion even though your
achievements are unparalleled, absolute
and cover all aspects of worldly
circulation and also reality. It spreads
happiness.

प्रभावती प्रभारूपा प्रसिद्धा परमेश्वरी ।

मूलप्रकृति-रव्यक्ता व्यक्ताव्यक्त-स्वरूपिणी ॥८६॥

Prabhaavathee prabhaaroopaa
prasiddhaa prarameshwaree

Moola prakruti: avyakthaa
vyakthaavyakhtha swaroopinee

Salutations to my Guru, Prabhavati Raje, former Princess of Devas M.P. India. Mother makes you radiant and glowing, widely known for your expertise in your field, highly active while always showing to be just like any other ordinary mortal.

व्यापिनी विविधाकारा विद्याऽविद्या-स्वरूपिणी ।
महाकामेश-नयन कुमुदाह्लाद -कौमुदी ॥८७॥

Vyaapinee vividhaakaaraa vidhyaa
avidhyaa swaroopinee

Mahaakaamesha nayana
kumudhaahlaadha kaumudhee

You are surrounded by all sorts of people
- knowledgable and ignorant. You instil
in them a desire to be nurtured and
achieved by righteous, practical and
satisfying manner.

भक्त-हार्द-तमो-भेद-भानुमद्भानु-सन्ततिः ।
शिवदूती शिवाराध्या शिवमूर्तिः-शिवङ्करी ॥८८॥

Bhaktha haardha thamobhedha
bhaanumadh bhaanusanthathi:

Shivadhoothee shivaaraadhyaa
shivamoorthi: shivankaree

She blesses you to dispel ignorance from
people around you, make them shine, get
mental peace and stay always happy.

शिवप्रिया शिवपरा शिष्टेष्टा शिष्टपूजिता ।
अप्रमेया स्वप्रकाशा मनो-वाचामगोचरा ॥८९॥

Shivapriyaa shivaparaa shishteshthaa sishthapoojithaa

Aprameyaa swaprakaashaa manovaachaa magocharaa

She blesses you to ever seek mental peace to do right things as prescribed by our elders. Your range of mind and speech are beyond judgement by normal standards, thus you are self illuminated by Her presence in you.

चिच्छक्ति-श्चेतना-रूपा जडशक्तिः - जडात्मिका ।
गायत्री व्याहृतिः सन्ध्या द्विजवृन्द-निषेविता ॥९०॥

Chit shakthi: chethanaa roopaa
jadashakthi: jadaathmikaa

Gaayathreevyaahruthi: sandhyaa dhwija
vrundha nishevithaa

Her blessings make you think before you
act. This ensures your work is based on
deep Knowledge and praised by experts.

तत्त्वासना तत्त्वमयी पञ्चकोशान्तर-स्थिता ।
निःसीम-महिमा नित्य-यौवना मदशालिनी ॥९१॥

Thathvaasanaa thathvamayee pancha
koshaanthara sthithaa

Nisseema mahimaa nithya youvanaa
madhasaalinee

You are adhering to the fact that She is
yourself. Hence you are one with nature,
fully enthusiastic, very young in spirit
and with boundless energy.

मदघूर्णित -रक्ताक्षी मदपाटल-गण्डभूः ।
चन्दन-द्रव-दिग्धाङ्गी चाम्पेय-कुसुम-प्रिया ॥९२॥

Madhaghoornitha rakthaakshee
madhapaatala gandabhoo:

Chandhana dhrava dhigdhaanghee
chaampeya kusumapriyaa

You express your full happiness through
your lively eyes. Your success is spread
across like fragrance of sandal powder or
champakaa flower, enjoyable by all.

कुशला कोमलाकारा कुरुकुल्ला कुलेश्वरी ।
कुलकुण्डालया कौलमार्गतत्पर सेविता ॥९३॥

Kushalaa komalaakaaraa kurukullaa kuleshwaree

Kulakundaalayaa kaula maarga thathpara sevithaa

Your chosen path, which your forefathers and ancestors have followed, is with full commitment to achieve your objectives and they all bless you to succeed.

कुमार गणनाथांबा तुष्टिः पुष्टि-मति-धृतिः ।
शान्तिः स्वस्तिमती कान्ति-नन्दिनी विघ्ननाशिनी ॥९४॥

Kumaara gananaathaambhaa thusthi:
pushthi: mathi: dhruthi:

Shaanthi: swasthimathee kaanthi:
nandhinee vighnanaashinee

You have the blessings of Lord Ganesha, Subramanya and Mother. Hence you will experience abundant happiness, growth, intelligence, courage, serenity, benevolent mental approach, brightness and overcome obstacles in any worldly activity.

तेजोवती त्रिनयना लोलाक्षी-कामरूपिणी ।
मालिनी हंसिनी माता मलयाचल-वासिनी ॥९५॥

Tejovathee thrinayanaa lolaakshee
kaamaroopinee

Maalinee hamsinee maathaa
malayaachala vaasinee

Mother ensures you to keep your mind
active and eyes watchful. This will bring
glory and fetch you bouquets and
garlands formed with rare and fragrant
hilly flowers.

सुमुखी नलिनी सुभ्रूःशोभना सुरनायिका ।
कालकण्ठी कान्तिमती क्षोभिणी सूक्ष्मरूपिणी ॥९६॥

Sumukhee nalinee subhroo: shobhanaa suranaayikaa

Kaalakantee kaanthimathee kshobhinee sookshmaroopinee

Your face shows divinity and you have leadership-quality, time consciousness, intolerance to wrong doing and your concern for minute details.

वज्रेश्वरी वामदेवी वयोऽवस्था विवर्जिता ।
सिद्धेश्वरी सिद्धविद्या सिद्धमाता यशस्विनी ॥९७॥

Vajreswaree vaamadhevee vayovasthaa vivarjithaa

Siddheswaree siddhavidhyaa siddhamaathaa yashaswinee

You are a strong and constant follower of the righteous path. You achieve fame by sheer intelligence due to Mother's grace.

विशुद्धिचक्र-निलया-ऽऽरक्तवर्णा त्रिलोचना ।
खट्वाङ्गादि-प्रहरणा वदनैक-समन्विता ॥९८॥

Vishuddhichakra nilayaa aarakthavarnaa thrilochanaa

Khadwaangaadhi praharanaa vadhanaika samanvithaa

You will achieve in the field of engineering, rotary machines, metal forming, lecturing and consultancy.

पायसान्न-प्रिया त्वक्स्था पशुलोक भयङ्करी ।
अमृतादि-महाशक्ति-संवृता डाकिनीश्वरी ॥९९॥

Payasaanna priyaa thwaksthaa
pashuloka bhayankaree

Amruthaadhi mahaashakthi samvruthaa
daagineeswaree

You can get involved in food industry,
animal husbandry, health and life saving
drugs and be successful.

अनाहताब्ज निलया श्यामाभा वदनद्वया ।
दंष्ट्रोज्ज्वलाऽक्षमालादिधरा रुधिरसंस्थिता॥१००॥

Anaahathaabhja nilayaa shyaamaabhaa
vadhanadhwayaa

Dhamshtrojwalaaksha maalaadhi dharaa
rudhira samsthithaa

All planets favour you to be specific on
any subject, offer clarity on topics of teeth
and blood related area.

कालरात्र्यादि- शक्त्यौघ-वृता स्निग्धौदन-प्रिया ।
महावीरेन्द्र-वरदा राकिण्यम्बा-स्वरूपिणी ॥१०१॥

Kaala rathryaadhi shakthyougha vruthaa
snighdhou dhana priyaa

Mahaa veerendhra varadhaa
raakinyambhaa swaroopinee

You will be surrounded by your close
people of different energy levels who are
experts in their related fields.

मणिपूराब्ज-निलया वदनत्रय-संयुता ।
वज्रादिकायुधोपेता डामर्यादिभिरावृता ॥१०२॥

Manipooraabhja nilayaa vadhanathraya samyuthaa

Vajraadhikaayudhopethaa daamaryaadhibhi: aavruthaa

With these valuable experts you can take up projects in military and protection equipments and accessories.

रक्तवर्णा मांसनिष्ठा गुडान्न-प्रीत-मानसा ।
समस्तभक्त-सुखदा लाखिन्यम्बा-स्वरूपिणी॥१०३॥

Rakthavarnaa maamsanishtaa gudaanna
preetha maanasaa

Samastha bhakthasukhadhaa
laakhinyambhaa swaroopinee

When your thoughts crystallise, they will
enter your flesh and blood as part of the
stream in your involved area. Your
confident approach will bring happiness
to all involved.

स्वादिष्टानांबुजगता चतुर्वक्त्र-मनोहरा ।
शूलाद्यायुध-सम्पन्ना पीतवर्णाऽतिगर्विता ॥१०४॥

Swaadhishtaanaambhujagathaa
chathurvakthra manoharaa

Shoolaadhyaayuudha sampannaa
peethavarnaa   athigarvithaa

Self control leads you to success, making people all around you happy. Your sharp and precise approach makes the people who interact with you proud to be involved with you.

मेदो-निष्ठा मधुप्रीता बन्धिन्याद्दि-समन्विता ।
दध्यन्नासक्त-हृदया काकिनी-रूप-धारिणी ॥१०५॥

Medhonishtaa madhupreethaa
bhandhinyaadhi samanvithaa

Dhadhyannaa sakhtha hrudhayaa
kaakinee roopa dhaarinee

With your knowledge fully imparted,
your relatives and friends who take to
alcohol and such habits excessively will
return to normalcy. You take on yourself
the protective role for them.

मूलाधाराम्बुजारूढा पञ्चवक्त्रास्थि संस्थिता ।
अङ्कुशादि-प्रहरणा वरदादि-निषेविता ॥१०६॥

Moolaadhara ambhujaaroodaa
panchavakhtraasthi samsthithaa

Ankushaadhi praharanaa varadhadhi
nishevithaa

You go into the roots of various activities
possible through different approaches
and guide the result of your work to
reach the people.

मुद्गौदनासक्त-चित्ता साकिन्यम्बा-स्वरूपिणी ।
आज्ञा-चक्राब्ज-निलयाशुक्लवर्णा षडानना ॥१०७॥

Mudhgoudhanaa saktha chitthaa
saakinyambaa swaroopinee

Aagyaa chakraabhja nilayaa
shuklavarnaa shadaananaa

Essential ingredients in your activity are
properly chosen by Her for you leading
to successful realisation. This caters to the
various requirements of all people and it
is simply remarkable.

मज्जा -संस्था हंसवती -मुख्य-शक्ति-समन्विता।
हरिद्रान्नैक-रसिका हाकिनी-रूप-धारिणी ॥१०८॥

Majjaa samsthaa hamsavathee mukhya
shakthi samanvithaa

Haridhraannaika rasikaa haakinee roopa
dharinee

Your activity will sail through different
areas with full energy and they will be
availed by people for their prosperity
and well being.

सहस्रदल-पद्मस्था सर्व-वर्णोप-शोभिता।
सर्वायुध-धरा शुक्ल-संस्थिता सर्वतोमुखी ॥१०९॥

Sahasradhala padhmasthaa sarvavarnopa shobhithaa

Sarvaayudha dharaa shuklasamsthithaa sarvathomukhee

Highly intricate but vast product range will come out through you successfully. They will have the assurance of performance and universal adaptability.

सर्वौदन-प्रीतचित्ता याकिन्यंबा -स्वरूपिणी ।
स्वाहा स्वधा मतिर्मेधा श्रुति-स्मृति-रनुत्तमा ॥११०॥

Sarvoudhana preetha chitthaa
yaakinyambhaa swaroopinee

Swaahaa swadhaa mathirmedhaa
shruthi smruthiranutthamaa

Your mind analyses and creates the procedure in the most natural form for others to follow in very easy way. This will be viewed in high esteem.

पुण्यकीर्तिः पुण्यलभ्या पुण्यश्रवण-कीर्तना ।
पुलोमजार्चिता बन्धमोचनी बर्बरालका ॥१११॥

Punyakeerthi: punyalabhyaa
punyashravana keerthanaa

Pulomajaarchithaa bandhamochanee
barbaraalakaa

Having implemented the new invention, you offer the procedure to people to free themselves from the bondage with the body and the mind.

विमर्शरूपिणी विद्‌या वियदादि-जगत्प्रसूः ।
सर्वव्याधि-प्रशमनी सर्वमृत्यु-निवारिणी ॥११२॥

Vimarsharoopinee vidhyaa viyadhaadhi jagathprasoo:

Sarvavyaadhi prashamanee sarva mruthyu nivaarinee

Being clear in your objective and with natural knowledge, you are blessed with a long healthy life that will automatically remove the fear of death.

अग्रगण्या-अचिन्त्यरूपा कलिकल्मष-नाशिनी।
कात्यायनी कालहन्त्री कमलाक्ष- निषेविता ॥११३॥

Agraganyaa achinthyaroopaa
kalikalmasha nashinee

Kaathyaayanee kaalahanthree
kamalaaksha nishevithaa

Being in the midst of intelligent people leading the way enables you to destroy all the negatives you encounter and emerge with glorious success.

ताम्बूल पूरित-मुखी दाडिमी कुसुम-प्रभा ।
मृगाक्षी मोहिनी मुख्या मृडानी मित्ररूपिणी ॥११४॥

Thaamboolapooritha mukhee dhadimee kusumaprabhaa

Mrugaakshee mohinee mukhyaa mrudaanee mithraroopinee

Ever energetic and fresh like a newly blossomed flower, you will be watchful with attractive eyes to spread happiness like soothing morning sunshine.

नित्य-तृप्ता भक्तनिधि-नियन्त्री निखिलेश्वरी ।
मैत्र्यादि वासनालभ्या महा-प्रलय-साक्षिणी ॥११५॥

Nithyathrupthaa bhakthanidhi: niyanthree nikhileshwaree

Maithryaadhi vaasanaalabhyaa mahaa pralaya saakshinee

You will be content and your friends will seek your guidance and have the desire to emulate your traits because you are seen to stand tall in any adverse situation.

पराशक्तिः परानिष्ठा प्रज्ञानघन-रूपिणी ।
माध्वीपानालसा मत्ता मातृका-वर्ण-रूपिणी ॥११६॥

Paraashakthi: paraanishttaa pragyaana ghanaroopinee

Maadhwee paanaalasaa matthaa mathrukaa varnaroopinee

You have vast energy and are committed to deep inner knowledge. You understand that all the communications and activities in the world are correlated to Her blessings and guidance

महाकैलास-निलया मृणाल- मृदु - दोर्लता ।
महनीया-दयामूर्ति-र्महा सामाज्य शालिनी ॥११७॥

Mahaakailaasa nilayaa mrunaala
mrudhu dhorlathaa

Mahaneeyaa dhayaa moorthi:
mahaasaamraajya shalinee

You are the centre of the peak of prayers
and meditation and with your soft hands
hold the world into a great place of
compassion and good people.

आत्मविद्‌या महाविद्‌या श्रीविद्‌या कामसेविता ।
श्रीषोडशाक्षरी विद्‌या त्रिकूटा कामकोटिका ॥११८॥

Aathma vidhyaa mahaavidhhyaa
Shreevidhyaa kaamasevithaa

Shreeshodasaaksharee vidhhyaa
trikootaa kaamakotikaa

Your realisation that Mother is seated in the blossomed flower of your Aatma peeta helps people through you to attain extreme happiness while practicing their daily activities.

कटाक्ष-किङ्करी-भूत-कमला कोटि-सेविता ।
शिरः स्थिता चन्द्रनिभा भालस्थेन्द्र-धनुः-प्रभा ॥११९॥

Kataaksha kinkareebhootha kamalaa koti sevithaa

Shira: sthithaa chandhranibhaa bhaalasthendhra dhanuprabhaa

Your attention bestows on everyone good wealth and pure beauty bringing their colourful personality to the fore for their benefit.

हृदयस्था रविप्रख्या त्रिकोणान्तर-दीपिका ।
दाक्षायणी दैत्यहन्त्री दक्षयज्ञविनाशिनी ॥१२०॥

Hrudhayasthaa raviprakhyaa
thrikonaandhara dheepikaa

Dhaakshaayanee daithyahanthree
dhaksha yagya vinaashinee

Mother makes you shine like the Sun, available to everyone in all direction. You destroy the impediments and tendencies obstructing good deeds which are highly valuable.

दरान्दोलित-दीर्घाक्षी दरहासोज्ज्वलन्मुखी ।
गुरु-मूर्ति-गुणनिधिः-गोमाता-गुहजन्म-भूः ॥१२१॥

Dharaandholitha dheerghaakshee
dharahaasojwalanmukhee

Gurumoorthi: guna nidhi: go maathaa
guhajanmabhoo:

People come to you for guidance to gain
knowledge in the form of caring and
meaningful words similar to a teacher to
his passionate students.

देवेशी दण्डनीतिस्था दहराकाश-रूपिणी ।
प्रतिपन्मुख्य-राकान्त-तिथि-मण्डल-पूजिता॥१२२॥

Dheveshee dhandaneethisthaa dhaharaakaasha roopinee

Prathipan mukhya raakaantha thithi mandalapoojithaa

As a leader, you explain to others the effects of bad deeds and show them the easy path to experience the reality. Efforts put at the right time will take you to good results.

कलात्मिका कलानाथा काव्यालाप-विनोदिनी ।
सचामर-रमा-वाणी सव्य दक्षिण-सेविता ॥१२३॥

Kalaathmikaa kalaanaathaa
kaavyaalaapa vinodhinee

Sachaamara ramaa vaanee
savyadhakshina sevithaa

You will be at the centre of all activities, your words pleasing and soothing. You are surrounded by learned and wealthy people to ensure their useful participation in your endeavour.

आदिशक्ति-रमेयात्मा परमा पावनाकृतिः ।
अनेक-कोटि-ब्रह्माण्ड-जननी दिव्य-विग्रहा ॥१२४॥

Aadhishakthi: ameyaathmaa paramaa paavanaakruthi:

Aneka koti brahmaanda jananee dhivya vigrahaa

Deriving the divine Tejas, you will provide motherly affection and attention to all the people. Because of your profound knowledge, purity in action and immeasurable energy, you will always guide people.

क्लींकारी केवला गुह्या कैवल्य-पद-दायिनी ।
त्रिपुरा त्रिजगद्वन्द्या त्रिमूर्ति–त्रिदशेश्वरी॥१२५॥

Kleenkaaree kevalaa guhyaa kaivalya
padha dhaayinee

Thripuraa thrijagadhvandhyaa
thrimoorthi: thridhasheshwaree

By Her presence in you, you are easily
approachable to the world of sadhus, the
wealthy and the poor. You are capable of
guiding the minds of all the three classes
of people.

त्र्यक्षरी दिव्य-गन्धाढ्या सिन्दूर-तिलकाञ्चिता ।
उमा शैलेन्द्रतनया गौरी गन्धर्व-सेविता ॥१२६॥

Thriyaksharee dhivaya gandhaadyaa
sindhoora thilakaanchithaa

Umaa shailendhra thanayaa gowree
gandharva sevithaa

Confidence, concentration and conquering are added to your fragrant glory. Even people from far flung hill locks come for guidance to attain happiness in life.

विश्वगर्भा स्वर्णगर्भा-ऽवरदा वागधीश्वरी ।
ध्यानगम्या-ऽपरिच्छेद्या ज्ञानदा ज्ञानविग्रहा ॥१२७॥

Viswagarbhaa swarnagarbhaa varadhaa vaagadheeswaree

Dhyaanagamyaa apariscchedhyaa gyaanadhaa gyaanavigrahaa

You will make people easily understand the facts of reality and priorities. You are good in meditation and have knowledge of the ultimate truth.

सर्व-वेदान्त-संवेद्या सत्यानन्द स्वरूपिणी ।
लोपामुद्रार्चिता लीलाक्लृप्त-ब्रह्माण्ड-मण्डला ॥१२८॥

Sarvavedhaantha samvedhyaa
sathyaanandha swaroopinee

Lopaamudhraarchithaa leela kluptha
brahmaanda mandalaa

You are fully aware regarding the source
of real happiness which is the essence of
all Vedas. You are blessed to perform
your chores smoothly.

अदृश्या दृश्यरहिता विज्ञात्री वेद्य-वर्जिता ।
योगिनी योगदा योग्या योगानन्दा युगन्धरा ॥१२९॥

Adhrushyaa dhrushyarahithaa
vigyaathree vedyavarjithaa

Yoginee yogathaa yogyaa yogaanandhaa
yugantharaa

The average human cannot understand
your identity with Mother. This is the
True Union worth exploring by people in
order to enjoy and through their own
practice, experience the lasting
happiness.

इच्छाशक्ति-ज्ञानशक्ति-क्रियाशक्ति-स्वरूपिणी ।
सर्वाधारा सुप्रतिष्ठा सदसद्रूप-धारिणी ॥१३०॥

Icchaa shakthi: gyaanashakthi: kriyaa
shakthi: swaroopinee

Sarvaadhaaraa suprathishtaa
sadhasathroopa dhaarinee

Your willpower, your setting of
objectives and the necessary action
culminate into total energy embodied in
you. Whether visible or not, foundation
gets fully laid.

अष्टमूर्ति-रजाजेत्री लोकयात्रा विधायिनी ।
एकाकिनी भूमरूपा निर्द्वैता द्वैतवर्जिता ॥१३१॥

Ashtamoorthi: rajaajethree lokayaathraa vidhaayinee

Ekaakinee bhoomaroopaa nirdhwaithaa dhwaithavarjithaa

In all the roles you take in your worldly activities, you see Mother and experience Her presence as the true activating force and also the only One.

अन्नदा वसुदा वृद्धा ब्रह्मात्मैक्य-स्वरूपिणी ।
बृहती ब्राह्मणी ब्राह्मी ब्रह्मानन्दा बलिप्रिया ॥१३२॥

Annadhaa vasudhaa vruddha
brahmaathmaikhya swaroopinee

Bruhathee braahmanee braahmee
brahmaanandhaa balipriyaa

You feed elders everywhere with
compassion. You will develop warm and
liberal outlook towards these people
helping them without expecting anything
in return.

भाषारूपा बृहत्सेना भावाभाव-विवर्जिता ।
सुखाराध्या शुभकरी शोभना सुलभागतिः ॥१३३॥

Bhaashaaroopaa bruhathsenaa
bhaavaabhaava vivarjithaa

Sukhaaraadhyaa shubhakaree shobhanaa
sulabhaagathi:

In achieving your objectives of doing good to humanity you receive help from learned people and derive satisfaction in the smooth way things happen.

राजराजेश्वरी राज्यदायिनी राज्यवल्लभा ।
राजत्कृपा राजपीठ-निवेशित- निजाश्रिता ॥१३४॥

Raajaraajeshwaree raajyadhaayinee
raajya vallabhaa

Raajathkrupaa raajapeeta niveshitha
nijaashrithaa

You make people participate in defined
area in your activity and they get
satisfaction due to their full involvement
as though it is their own.

राज्यलक्ष्मीः कोशनाथा चतुरङ्ग-बलेश्वरी ।
साम्राज्य-दायिनी सत्यसन्धा सागरमेखला॥१३५॥

Raajyalakshmee: Koshanaathaa
Chathuranga baleshwaree

Saamraajya dhaayinee sathyasandhaa
saagaramekhalaa

As you are aware of the functioning of
your body, the vast ocean of life is an
enjoyable experience to you due to Her
blessings.

दीक्षिता दैत्यशमनी सर्वलोकवशङ्करी ।
सर्वार्थदात्री सावित्री सच्चिदानन्द-रूपिणी ॥१३६॥

Dheekshithaa daithyashamanee
sarvaloka vashankaree

Sarvaarthadhathree saavithree
satchidhaanandha roopinee

You take a vow to remove all evil effects
and people become aware of their exact
necessities in life, and the required
energy to get them and also to get real
bliss.

देशकाला परिच्छिन्ना सर्वगा सर्वमोहिनी ।
सरस्वती शास्त्रमयी गुहाम्बा गुह्यरूपिणी ॥१३७॥

Dhesakaalaa paricchinnaa sarvagaa sarvamohinee

Saraswathee shaasthramayee guhaambhaa guhya roopinee

You enjoy the inner control which has no limitations, since you respect and follow old and ancient teachings already set in your brain.

सर्वोपाधि-विनिर्मुक्ता सदाशिव-पतिव्रता ।
संप्रदायेश्वरी साध्वी गुरुमण्डल-रूपिणी ॥१३८॥

Sarvopaadhi vinirmukhthaa sadhaashiva pathivrathaa

Sampradhaayeshwaree saadhwee gurumandala roopinee

You are devoted to peace and show respect for all those traditional values which are relevant today and easily practiceable.

कुलोत्तीर्णा भगाराध्या माया मधुमती मही ।
गणाम्बा गुह्यकाराध्या कोमलाङ्गी गुरुप्रिया ॥१३९॥

Kulotheernaa bhagaaraadhyaa maayaa
madhumathee mahee

Ganaambhaa guhyakaaraadhyaa
komalaangee gurupriya

You will resist temptations, which your
gurus and teachers appreciate. It is easy
to understand and then practice and that
is the proper way.

स्वतन्त्रा सर्वतन्त्रेशी दक्षिणामूर्ति-रूपिणी ।
सनकादि-समाराध्या शिवज्ञान-प्रदायिनी ॥१४०॥

Swathanthraa sarwathanthreshee
dhakshinaamoorthi roopinee

Sanakaadhi samaaraadhyaa shivagyaana
pradhaayinee

Though all your limbs are totally
independently acting, they always act in
unison due to GURU's blessings and you
will impart this knowledge and practice
to the needy.

चित्कलाऽऽनन्द-कलिका प्रेमरूपा प्रियङ्करी ।
नामपारायण -प्रीता नन्दिविद्या नटेश्वरी ॥१४१॥

Chithkalaa aanandha kalikaa
premaroopaa priyankaree

Naamapaaraayana preethaa
nandhividhyaa nateswaree

Mental agility, love, affection and happiness will increase multi fold by chanting of these mantra and your enthusiasm grows to very rosy heights, your ears will hear pleasing sounds and words.

मिथ्या-जगदधिष्ठाना मुक्तिदा मुक्तिरूपिणी ।
लास्यप्रिया लयकरी लज्जा रम्भादिवन्दिता ॥१४२॥

Mithyaa jagadhadhishtaana mukthidhaa
mukthiroopinee

Laasya priyaa layakaree lajjaa
rambhaadhi vadhithaa

By Her grace you will correct others'
wrongly placed faith on non relevant
understanding. Due to this you will be
respected by one and all.

भवदाव-सुधावृष्टिः पापारण्य-दवानला ।
दौर्भाग्य-तूलवातूला जराध्वान्तरविप्रभा ॥१४३॥

Bhavadhaava sudhaavrushti:
paapaaranya dhavaanalaa

Dhourbhaagya thoolavaathoolaa
jaraadhvaantha raviprabhaa

You can guide people to enjoy continuous flow of prosperity in the present and for their future generations by showing them ways to eliminate sins and misdeeds.

भाग्याब्धि-चन्द्रिका भक्त-चित्त-केकि- घनाघना ।
रोगपर्वत-दम्भोलि-मृत्युदारु-कुठारिका ॥१४४॥

Bhaagyaabhdhi chandhrikaa bhaktha chittha keki ghanaaghanaa

Rogaparvatha dhambholi: mruthyudhaaru kutaarikaa

Your enthusiasm is like an energetic wave of fortune to all benevolent humans. You are like the rain bearing cloud. You eradicate all diseases and take away the fear of death.

महेश्वरी महाकाली महाग्रासा महाशना ।
अपर्णा चण्डिका चण्ड मुण्डासुर-निषूदिनी ॥१४५॥

Maheshwaree mahaakaalee
mahaagraasaa mahaashanaa

Aparnaa chandikaa chanda mundaasura
nishoodhinee

You will sacrifice food, comfort and work
relentlessly till you destroy all sins, and
avoid bad deeds and bad thoughts.

क्षराक्षरात्मिका सर्वलोकेशी विश्वधारिणी ।
त्रिवर्गदात्री सुभगा त्र्यम्बका त्रिगुणात्मिका ॥१४६॥

Ksharaaksharaathmikaa sarvalokeshee
vishwadhaarinee

Thrivargadhaathree subhagaa
thryambakaa thrigunaathmikaa

You solve problems of others without
compromising your principles. You offer
solution acceptable to all.

स्वर्गापवर्गदा शुद्धा जपापुष्प-निभाकृतिः ।
ओजोवती द्युतिधरा यज्ञरूपा प्रियव्रता ॥१४७॥

Swargaapavargadhaa shuddhaa
japaapushpa nibhaakruthi:

Ojovathee dhyuthidharaa yagyaroopaa
priyavrathaa

With Mother's presence active in your life
you will enjoy eternal bliss. You will
have a life full of energy, eloquence and
divinity

दुराराध्या दुराधर्षा पाटली-कुसुम-प्रिया।
महती मेरुनिलया मन्दार कुसुम-प्रिया॥१४८॥

Dhuraaraadhyaa dhuraadharshaa
paatalee kusumapriyaa

Mahathee merunilayaa mandhaara
kusumapriyaa

You exude fragrance and contentment. People who do not have control over their senses will never become part of you.

वीराराध्या विराड्रूपा विरजा विश्वतोमुखी ।
प्रत्यग्-रूपा पराकाशा प्राणदा प्राणरूपिणी ॥१४९॥

Veeraaraadhyaa viraadroopaa virajaa
vishwathomukhee

Prathyagroopaa paraakaashaa
praanadhaa praanaroopinee

By Mother's blessings you are
blemishless, you have a broad outlook
and you create a better environment all
around you because of the effect of your
inner vision.

मार्ताण्ड-भैरवाराध्या मन्त्रिणी-न्यस्त-राज्यधूः ।
त्रिपुरेशी जयत्सेना निस्त्रैगुण्या परापरा ॥१५०॥

Maarthaanda bhairavaaraadhyaa manthrinee nyastha raajyadhoo:

Thripureshee jayathsenaa nisthraigunyaa paraaparaa

Extremely poor section of the society looks for guidance to earn their livelihood, security and happiness. You will provide this to them and help them lead a better life.

सत्यज्ञानानन्द –रूपा सामरस्य परायणा ।
कर्पर्दिनी कलामाला कामधु-क्काम-रूपिणी ॥१५१॥

Sathyagyaanaa aanandharoopaa
saamarasya paraayanaa

Kapardhinee kalaamaalaa kaamadhuk
kaamaroopinee

With your adherence to truth knowledge
and happiness you are strong and will
achieve your desires by balancing all
aspects of life.

कलानिधिः काव्यकला रसज्ञा रसशेवधिः ।
पुष्टा पुरातना पूज्या पुष्करा पुष्करेक्षणा ॥५२॥

Kalaanidhi: kaavyakalaa rasagyaa rasashevadhi:

Pushtaa puraathanaa poojyaa pushkaraa pushkarekshanaa

You are explicit and give expert views. You lead people to have inner vision on that Pure and Total energy form, the Mother. It makes them follow all old customs whose values are fully relevant in current times.

परंज्योतिः परंधाम परमाणुः परात्परा ।
पाशहस्ता पाशहन्त्री परमन्त्र-विभेदिनी ॥१५३॥

Paramjyothi: paramdhaama paramaanu:
paraathparaa

Paashahasthaa pashahanthree
paramanthra vibhedhinee

Mother is affectionate, compassionate
and removes all the mental confusion.
She is the illumination in totality, both
finite and infinite.

मूर्ताऽमूर्ता ऽनित्यतृप्ता मुनिमानस-हंसिका ।
सत्यव्रता सत्यरूपा सर्वान्तर्यामिनी सती ॥१५४॥

Moorthaamoorthaa   anithyathrupthaa
munimaanasa hamsikaa

Sathyavrathaa sathyaroopaa
sarvaantharyaaminee sathee

You realise She is active through you.
You are not looking for
acknowledgement or appreciation for
your work. People realise your
achievements by interacting with you.

ब्रह्माणी ब्रह्मजननी बहुरूपा बुधार्चिता ।
प्रसवित्री प्रचण्डाऽऽज्ञा प्रतिष्ठा प्रकटाकृतिः ॥१५५॥

Brahmaanee Brahmajananee bahuroopaa
bhudhaarchithaa

Prasavithree prachandaagyaa prathishtaa
prakataakruthi:

The Universality of Mother is in all
people of various creed and color spread
across in all of you as the fully
established truth.

प्राणेश्वरी प्राणदात्री पञ्चाशत्पीठ-रूपिणी।
विश्रृङ्खला विविक्तस्था वीरमाता वियत्प्रसूः ॥१५६॥

Praaneshwaree praanadhathree
panchaasathpeeta roopinee

Vishrunkalaa vivikthashthaa
veeramaathaa viyathprasoo:

The air gets cleared of all impurities by
chanting of the stotram after installing
Her in the Aatma Peetam. This is the
way all ascetic and learned people
worship.

मुकुन्दा मुक्तिनिलया मूलविग्रह -रूपिणी ।
भावज्ञा भवरोगघ्नी भवचक्र-प्रवर्तिनी ॥१५७॥

Mukundhaa mukthinilayaa
moolavigraha roopinee

Bhaavagyaa bhavarogagnee bhavachakra
pravarthinee

Mother helps you to free from all bonds,
due to which you will lead a life full of
good health and knowledge.

छन्दः सारा शास्त्रसारा मन्त्रसारा तलोदरी ।
उदारकीर्ति-रुद्दामवैभवा वर्णरूपिणी ॥१५८॥

Cchandhassaaraa shaasthrasaaraa
manthrasaaraa thalodharee

Udhaarakeerthiruddhaama vaibhavaa
varnaroopinee

You are in proximity to all the elders who
are learned in the scriptures. You have
strong control of the mind.This is
possible because of your realisation that
you are one with Her.

जन्ममृत्यु-जरातप्त-जन-विश्रान्ति-दायिनी ।
सर्वोपनिष-दुद्घुष्टा शान्त्यतीत-कलात्मिका ॥१५९॥

Janmamruthyu jaraathaptha Jana
vishraanthi dhaayinee

Sarvopanishadhudhgushtaa
shanthyatheetha kalaathmikaa

All the physical and mental problems
happening during the period of birth and
death, particularly in your old age will
disappear and you are at permanent
peace experiencing Her from within.

गंभीरा गगनान्तस्था गर्विता गानलोलुपा ।
कल्पना-रहिता काष्ठा ऽकान्ता कान्तार्ध-विग्रहा ॥१६०॥

Ghambheeraa gaganaanthasthaa
garvithaa gaanalolupaa

Kalpanaa rahithaa kaashtaa kaanthaa
kaanthaardha vigrahaa

For the control of the mind you should have peace and harmony. This is possible because She is the sole source of your strength and ensures your happiness at all times.

कार्यकारण-निर्मुक्ता कामकेलि-तरंगिता ।
कनत्कनक-ताटङ्का लीला-विग्रह-धारिणी ॥१६१॥

Kaaryakaarana nirmukthaa kaamakeli tharangithaa

Kanathkanaka thaatankaa leelaa vigraha dhaarinee

Cause and effect on any action will not affect you since you realise you are the tool and She is the actuator.

अजा क्षयविनिर्मुक्ता मुग्धा क्षिप्र-प्रसादिनी ।
अन्तर्मुख-समाराध्या बहिर्मुख सुदुर्लभा ॥१६२॥

Ajaa kshaya vinirmukhthaa mugdhaa
kshipra prasaadhinee

Antharmukha samaaraadhyaa
bahirmukha sudhurlabhaa

She is very difficult to be seen outside but
resides (inside you) and is available for
your inner vision. This inner vision
instantly removes all your mistakes and
difficulties.

त्रयी त्रिवर्ग –निलया त्रिस्था त्रिपुर-मालिनी ।
निरामया निरालम्बा स्वात्मारामा सुधासृतिः ॥१६३॥

Thrayee thrivarganilayaa thristhaa
thripura maalinee

Niraamayaa niraalambaa
swathmaaraamaa sudhasruthi:

She provides continuous joy and
prosperity for those who recognise Her
presence inside them and concentrate
with unified mind and body on Her.

संसारपङ्क-निर्मग्न-समुद्धरण-पण्डिता ।
यज्ञ-प्रिया यज्ञकर्त्री यजमान-स्वरूपिणी॥१६४॥

Samsaara pankha nirmagna
samuddharana pandithaa

Yagyapriyaa yagya karthree yajamaana
swaroopinee

You can overcome tensions of life and the
fear of death if you have a firm resolution
to achieve what you plan.

धर्माधारा धनाध्यक्षा धनधान्य-विवर्धिनी ।
विप्रप्रिया विप्ररूपा विश्वभ्रमण-कारिणी॥१६५॥

Dharmaadhaaraa dhanaadhyakshaa
dhana dhaanya vivardhinee

Viprapriyaa vipraroopaa vishwa
bramana kaarinee

People have to make money for food and existence in righteous way and make it grow. They should be liked by knowledgeable people who will be blessed to go around the world on a purpose.

विश्वग्रासा विद्रुमाभा वैष्णवी विष्णुरूपिणी ।
अयोनिः योनि-निलया कूटस्था कुलरूपिणी ॥१६६॥

Viswagraasaa vidhrumaabhaa vaishnavee vishnuroopinee

Ayoni: yoninilayaa kootasthaa kularoopinee

You will achieve the inner vision by this method of mental concentration than by means of traditional methods.

वीरगोष्ठी-प्रिया वीरा नैष्कर्म्या नादरूपिणी ।
विज्ञानकलना कल्या निदग्धा बैन्दवासना ॥१६७॥

Veeragoshtee priyaa veeraa
naishkarmyaa naadha roopinee

Vigyaana kalanaa kalyaa nidhagdhaa
baindhavaasanaa

Through various forms of actions, you
and your associates will work on all the
details of the excercise and activity with
full concentration.

तत्वाधिका तत्वमयी तत्त्वमर्थ-स्वरूपिणी ।
सामगान-प्रिया सौम्या सदाशिव-कुटुम्बिनी ॥१६८॥

Thathwaadhikaa thathwamayee
thathwamartha swaroopinee

Saamagaana priyaa saumya sadhaashiva
kutumbinee

You all experience the ultimate Truth and
develop people who will understand
they are part of the universal divine
family and so practice peace with
confidence

सव्यापसव्य-मार्गस्था सर्वापद्विनिवारिणी ।
स्वस्था स्वभावमधुरा धीरा धीरसमर्चिता ॥१६९॥

Savyaapasavya maargasthaa
sarvaapadhvi nivaarinee

Swasthaa swabhaava madhuraa dheeraa
dheera samarchithaa

By nature, we are all endowed with
knowledge to tread in a path without any
difficulty or danger. This is proven by
men of true wisdom, courage and
confidence and sweet behaviour by
nature.

चैतन्यार्घ्य-समाराध्या चैतन्य-कुसुम-प्रिया ।
सदोदिता सदातुष्टा तरुणादित्य-पाटला ॥१७०॥

Chaithanyaarghya samaaraadhyaa
chaithanya kusuma priyaa

Sadhodhithaa sadhaa thushtaa
tharunaadhithya paatalaa

Mental concentration facilitates
brightness like the early morning sun and
gives full happiness all the time. It is the
aspirations of people who are fickle
minded and want to improve by learning
from you.

दक्षिणा-दक्षिणाराध्या दरस्मेर-मुखाम्बुजा ।
कौलिनी-केवलाऽनर्घ्य-कैवल्य-पद-दायिनी ॥१७१॥

Dhakshinaa dhakshinaaraadhyaa
darasmera mukhaambujaa

Koulinee kevalaanargya kaivalya padha
dhaayinee

When the ignorant and the unlearned
people see the smiling face of the Mother
they feel She is close to their family and
hence belongs to them. This gives them
confidence that she will protect them.

स्तोत्र-प्रिया स्तुतिमती श्रुति-संस्तुत-वैभवा।
मनस्विनी मानवती महेशी मङ्गलाकृतिः ॥ १७२ ॥

Sthothra priyaa sthuthimathee sruthi
samsthutha vaibhavaa

Manasvinee maanavathee maheshee
mangalaakruthi:

People who chant the stotra with dedication and involvement, who practise to their full capabilities and knowledge, get to see Her in Her full grandeur form.

विश्वमाता जगद्धात्री विशालाक्षी विरागिणी
प्रगल्भा परमोदारा परामोदा मनोमयी ॥१७३॥

Viswamaathaa jagath dhaathree vishaalaakshee viraaginee

Pragalbaa paramodhaaraa paraamodhaa manomayee

The mother looks after you with so much care and generosity that instills confidence in you, giving you the eternal bliss and activating you towards realisation.

व्योमकेशी विमानस्था वज्रिणी वामकेश्वरी ।
पञ्चयज्ञ-प्रिया पञ्च-प्रेत मञ्चाधिशायिनी ॥१७४॥

Vyomakeshee vimaanasthaa vajrinee vaamakeshwaree

Pancha yagya priyaa pancha pretha manchaadhishaayinee

Mother has dark hair synonymous to rain bearing clouds showing you that she is ready to shower blessings and prosperity on you. She controls the five Gunas influencing the mind and the body thereby bringing all the five elements of Nature within your command.

पञ्चमी पञ्चभूतेशी पंचसंख्योपचारिणी।
शाश्वती शाश्वतैश्वर्या शर्मदा शम्भुमोहिनी ॥१७५॥

Panchamee panchabhooteshee pancha
samkhyopa chaarinee

Shaashwathee shaahshwataishwaryaa
sharmadhaa shambhumohinee

She is the controlling force for the five
elements of Nature and the five Gunas,
influencing the behaviour of people. Her
corrective action gives us permanent
happiness in life with peace and
harmony.

धरा धरसुता धन्या धर्मिणी धर्मवर्धिनी ।
लोकातीता गुणातीता सर्वातीता शमात्मिका ॥१७६॥

Dharaa dharasuthaa dhanyaa dharminee dharmavardhinee

Lokaatheethaa gunaatheethaa sarvaatheethaa shamaathmikaaa

She instills in you patience, tolerance, gratefulness, righteousness and developing positive attitude. You will spread this across different regions, cultures and people and guide them all.

बन्धूक-कुसुम प्रख्या बाला लीला विनोदिनी ।
सुमङ्गली सुखकरी सुवेषाढ्या सुवासिनी ॥७७॥

Bandhooka kusumaprakhyaa baalaa leelaa vinodhinee

Sumangalee sukhakaree suveshaadyaa suvaasinee

Appreciating the positives and ignoring the negative actions of people, you will make all the people happy with good clothes and enthusiasm. You enrich everybody's life including the life of the children. You teach proper behaviour to the children in a playful way.

सुवासिन्यर्चन-प्रीताऽऽशोभना शुद्ध –मानसा ।
बिन्दु-तर्पण-संतुष्टा पूर्वजा त्रिपुराम्बिका॥१७८॥

Suvaasinyarchanapreethaa shobhanaa
suddha maanasaa

Bindhu tharpana samthushtaa poorvajaa
thripuraambikaa

People become blessed with good and
meaningful life, are able to speak with
pure mind and brightness. When we
successfully fulfil the core needs of our
activity we are able to view our past,
present and the future.

दशमुद्रा-समाराध्या त्रिपुरा श्रीवशङ्करी ।
ज्ञानमुद्रा ज्ञानगम्या ज्ञान-ज्ञेय-स्वरूपिणी ॥१७९॥

Dhashamudhraa samaaraadhyaa
thripuraa shree vashankaree

Gyaanamudhraa gyaanagamyaa gyaana
gyeya swaroopinee

Mother controls your desire, knowledge
and action. All your finger movements
in different forms denote your devotion
to Her. You thus receive deep and
thorough knowledge to see yourself in
Her.

योनिमुद्रा त्रिखण्डेशी त्रिगुणऽम्बा त्रिकोणगा ।
अनघाऽऽद्भुत-चारित्र वाच्छितार्थ- प्रदायिनी ॥१८०॥

Yonimudhraa thrikandeshee
thrigunaambaa thrikonagaa

Anaghaadhbhutha chaarithra
vaanchithaartha pradhaayinee

The three Gunas in you get correctly
oriented and aligned to the individual's
life activity.With this she grants you
preparation to mentally recognise that
you and She are the same.

अभ्यासातिशय-ज्ञाता षडध्वातीत-रूपिणी ।
अव्याज-करूणा-मूर्ति-रज्ञान-ध्वान्त दीपिका ॥१८१॥

Abhyaasaathishaya gyatha
shadadhvaatheethaa roopinee

Avyaaja karunaa moorthy: agyaana
dhwaantha deepikaa

She says "by constant practice and
concentration, you will realise me. You
may adopt any route but you will reach
me". She shows compassion
unequivocally since it is Her nature. She
is the beacon of brightness that removes
the darkness of ignorance.

आबाल-गोप-विदिता सर्वानुल्लंघ्य-शासना ।
श्रीचक्रराज-निलया श्रीमत्त्रिपुरसुन्दरी ॥१८२॥

Aabaala gopa vidhithaa
sarvaanullanghya shaasanaa

Shree chakraraaja nilayaa shreemath
thripurasundaree

Even a child or a labourer can realise
Her, the only requirement being
yearning, learning and practicing to see
Her seated in their Aathma Peeta the
peetam being in every one of us, with
the application of mental concentration.

श्रीशिवा शिव- शक्त्यैक्य -रूपिणी ललिताम्बिका ॥१८३॥

Shree shiva shakthi aikhya roopinee lalithaambikaa

Our potential capacity and flow of energy should be synchronised to enjoy the eternal bliss of vision of Mother seated inside us.

ஸ்ரீபாலாம்பிகை